the heart that silence built

the heart that silence built

poems about adoption, trauma, permanency, and family.

Wendy Louise Hayes

Published by Tablo

Table of Contents

beginnings

"Sometimes beginnings aren't so simple
Sometimes goodbye's the only way,"
- Shadow of the Day, Linkin Park

This book is a collection of poems that I wrote between the ages of 12 and 30. Each poem selected revolves around my adoption journey and was curated as an act of a radical unsilencing.

Appropriately, the first two poems in this book are two of the very first poems I ever wrote. This is appropriate for a couple of reasons. For one, publishing this book has been a part of my adoption healing journey. Second, I started writing in the fall of 2003, which was the year my sister was born. I turned 12 five days after she was born. My sister's birth would become a catalyst for many of our life experiences, including our adoption.

She is more at the center of this story than I am.

One of the things I wrestled with in envisioning this book was how much of my story to tell in a narrative way that includes timelines and details. I've included little spurts of explanation here and there to complement certain pieces, but overall, I want this work to stand on its own.

Part of my healing journey has been reclaiming myself from emotional abuse and gaslighting. So I created this book as an exercise and meditation on those experiences. What was interesting to me was that, during the process of looking back through my writing, I experienced so much validation. In retrospect I am grateful for these poems, even if I don't think all of them are 'good'. Which is why they are featured all the same. To honour my inner child and her experiences.

And if any of them can make you feel less alone in that "one weirdly specific adoption thing that nobody else seems to get," well, that's something too.

So thank you reader, for opening your heart to my healing. I think I've needed a little extra help carrying the burden.

This book comes with a playlist: The Heart That Silence Built. Find it on Spotify or at www.heartthatsilencebuilt.ca if you are interested. Lyrics from songs on this playlist are featured throughout the book.

Want to get in touch? heartthatsilencebuilt@gmail.com

"

Special thank-you to the generosity of my Dad, for supporting the publishing of this book as my graduation gift. This will allow me to use the proceeds of these sales toward my future schooling as I work towards becoming a psychotherapist.

A portion of the profits of this poetry book will also be donated to the Never Too Late Youth Connections Network. Thank you for being a generous supporter in community by purchasing this book. adoption.on.ca/ntl

pain

to cry

is to hurt

with the pain and grief

inside yourself

when your heart beats within your chest

and drops of blood leave stains and scars

and in your breath

it can be heard

within your heart

and you hear it beat

with every step

from your feet

it lives for ever

wondering

i wonder what god has in store for me

if i'll go home tonight or tomorrow

where all my friends are and if they're hurting

and who is calling on the phone

i wonder if death is as good as living

or if all my hard days will come in handy

the clock is ticking

and wasting my life

it's so weird how i can watch it go by

and every second or penny

really does count

oh how i wonder

if the grass is really greener

on the other side

"

I vividly remember writing this while my baby sister slept on the couch next me. I was wondering what she was thinking about, or how babies even did think without words.

sibling baby (before loss)

this moment is so perfect
i just can't explain
the sun is shining down
no room left for pain

she is smiling at me
i am smiling back
she is so beautiful
that's a true fact

there's nothing in the world
that could make me this happy
not riches, not fame
i kind of feel like laughing

this is so weird
i'm not used to this type of love
it's so unconditional
nothing makes it rough

intermission

this...funeral
that nobody would call a funeral
that nobody would let me mourn or scream or cry or just
end.

~

There are critical moments in time that shape us. Moments like scars that we trace with our "what-ifs..."

My sister and I were apprehended in 2004 and placed in the same foster home together. In 2006, I was told that they were looking for a family to take care of my sister. That this family might not want me, and I should "prepare myself" to lose her.

There is a moment that I remember writing about, but can't seem to find any poems about. I return to my foster home after being away at a week of camp. I call out, but no one is there. I drop my stuff at the door, because it's heavy and I'm tired. When I walk into the dining room, I see a photo album. Curiously, I open the photo album to see a lovely family with a golden retriever. The caption guts me, alone, in the house...my sister is probably with these people right now...

mom, dad, brother, dog

This was her new family.

HER new family.

There was no room for me in this picture.

They looked...*happy.*

What follows are poems primarily written in 2006, the year she was taken from me. When I didn't know that I would end up being with her again the following year. What a devastating year it was, I was 15. Yet, no one likes to talk about it. I guess because it ended up being "such a great story" for those on the outside looking in.

Which seemed to be everyone but me.

Reading and re-experiencing these poems has been difficult, but I am better for it. Healing takes work, and that means facing up to things people have tried to bury and silence.

i am

i am strong and beautiful
i wonder what death is like
i hear silence
i see nothingness
i want peace
i am strong and beautiful

i pretend i am somewhere else
i feel lonely
i worry about losing faith
i touch heaven
i cry for freedom
i am strong and beautiful

i understand pain
i say hold on
i dream of peace
i try to do better
i hope everything works out
i am strong and beautiful

dave

it's so weird to know
that i'll never see him again

even though i knew him only a short while
it was enough time to know

that he was a kind man
big hearted and generous

he was funny and easy to talk to
and always a fellow rocker.

but still don't feel sorry for him.
i know he's happy where he is

don't feel sorry for me
he was in my life

feel sorry for all those people
who never even got to shake his hand.

❝

*At my Children's Aid, we had volunteer drivers. Essentially it was a
group of people that volunteered to drive young people in child welfare
around to appointments and visits when the foster parent or worker
was not able to. I was always taken to my visits this way. On occasion,*

my volunteer driver would cancel and no one else would bring me to see my mom when that happened.

I formed a special bond with most of the volunteer drivers I had. Many of them took the time to listen to my poetry. Dave was special because he drove my sister and I together.

It's amazing how much one opens up on frequent drives.

Dave became a father figure in my life (my biological dad did not have an active role in my life at the time, and my foster dad was a real piece of work).

I want you to remember Dave, because after he passed away, his brother Dan started driving me, and there is a poem about him later in this book. Interestingly, I wrote Dan's poem before re-discovering this one. The poem I wrote for Dan was one of the major driving factors in deciding to publish this book.

not coming home?

she's not coming home.

she's not coming home?
what do you mean she is not coming home?
i've know for a month
but it just sunk in now

she's not coming home
but it just hit me
right here
in the middle of class

she's not coming home

i'm going to cry
my eyes are watering
right here
in the middle of class
i'm going to cry

i shoot my hand into the air
ask to go to the washroom
run down the hall
burst into a stall
and cry
just cry

oh my god.
she's not coming home

the pieces

where are the pieces?
the pieces missing from my heart
the ones scattered on the floor
they're blowing away
i can't see them anymore
and now there are pieces missing
how can i live without the pieces?
i'm like an old puzzle
where half the pieces are missing
and no one wants it anymore
there goes some more pieces
just floating away in the wind
like feathers of a bird
a bird cant fly without its feathers
so how can i live without my pieces?
there is one left
maybe if i hang on
it will last me
until i find more pieces
or i make new ones
but i will always treasure
the last piece
of my heart

my everything

you were everything,
everything i had.

when you left,
everything went with you.

now there is nothing,
nothing here and now.

what's the point,
if everything is with you?

can i hang on long enough,
to see everything with you again?

you are everything,
everything I have.

love and mistakes

you say that you are a bad mom
because of your mistakes
nobody is perfect
you must know this in your heart
and i know that you've done wrong
i know that you caused pain
not just upon myself
but nobody is perfect
and i will always love you
yes, no matter what
and I can name the best thing you've ever done
you loved
you care about my sister and me
that is more than i could ever ask
that makes you so amazing
no matter what you say
there are those out there that could care less
and even though you have made mistakes
you are still my mom and i will still love you
because you have always loved me.

she never is

every time I wake-up
and turn to
where she used to sleep
and pray
and hope
that when i open my eyes
she will be there
lost in her dreams

she never is

every night i go to my room
and i'm quiet as a mouse
so she'll stay asleep
and pray
and hope
that i won't wake her up
but she is not there sleeping

she never is

the end

The misconception is often that adoption is the happy ending...

palm trees

there's no way to express
what you've done for me
the things i thought i lost
that thing i wanted to be

you pulled me off the ground
and you gave me my wings
took me out of the dark
i owe you everything

you made me realize
that life can be worth living
that there is true love somewhere
love that just keeps on giving

when i thought all was lost
it was you i found
that everything is with it
after you've hit the ground

you carry me higher
make me feel like i deserve
the happiness i long for
solace in just 3 words

3 words that were dead
had become nothing to me
suddenly having meaning
after a couple of palm trees

there's no turning back

now that i finally feel wanted
there is happiness out there
a place that i won't feel haunted

"

Unfortunately, those who know...know love is not enough.

silence

"Your silence will not protect you."

Audre Lorde

~

One of the reasons I shy away from narratively explaining these experiences is because in many ways, it's almost more difficult to grasp them this way. Also, this book was not an exercise in helping people to understand, but in reaching out to those who already do.

The family that adopted my sister would eventually ask me to move in with them. They became my family as well. My 16th birthday would be celebrated in this new family, in this new life. Siblings staying together, older child adoption. Sounds like great news, right?

Maybe from the outside looking in.

Silence would became the permeating theme of this relationship, and my adoption/permanency journey. My sister's adoption was legally 'closed' - whatever that means. Closed is a funny word to me in this context. As if the outside world ceases to exist just because a door is closed.

My adoption was neither legal nor closed, and I would soon learn that who I am, my thoughts, values, experiences, beliefs and relationships would not be welcome in my new family.

Sharing these poems is a way of breaking that silence.

love

trembling **cold**
in a home you call love
i always imagined love to feel

warm?

won't understand

you don't see it
but i feel it
the glass wall between us
perhaps it was i who built it

and i bang
and i scream
and i cry
but you don't hear me or notice

and eventually i fall to my knees
so frustrated
that you don't understand

your pretty life mocks my hand-me-down clothes
you can't even comprehend the memories which haunt me
you just don't understand

my being longs for your attention
for the little things you seem to miss
you talk so big, but walk so small
and you just don't get it at all

i realize i'm no perfection
and i also realize i'm not ready
because you just don't understand

it hurts so much
that you just won't understand...
...you just won't understand

see beyond

does anybody see me?

well of course they can see me
but does anybody really understand seeing me?
every time someone looks at me
i don't understand the emotion

is that because you don't really see me?
am i just another person?
just another ideal?
just someone else to compare with?

accusation
expectance
disappointment

that is what i see
you think i'm just some other kid
some other under-achiever
some other teen who just doesn't care right?

hello!
hello!

there is a person beyond this physical tie-in
i'm not just some flesh and bone
a brain and a sac of organs

do I look like some kind of robot?
did you ever once think that maybe i am trying?
i have feelings too you know.

i'm going through more than what you see on the surface

and i'm sorry if
you just expect me to spill every emotion out to you
am i another disappointment?

did you ever think that maybe
my look is faltering
'cause i'm about to cry

did you ever think that maybe
you were applying too much pressure
and i'm fighting back the tears

did you ever think that maybe
i'm not ready to grow up
and move on yet

what's wrong with the look on my face?

hello!
hello!

am I so old
that i'm no long allowed to display emotion
where was the cut off age?
where are the rules?
why is it so wrong to just be what i want to be?
why is it so wrong to believe what i believe?

maybe i don't want to change for you...

untruthful

is there no truth
left within the world
what has my life come to
when i don't believe a word

i find myself debating
if it's all a lie
what's the point in living?
when all i do is cry

when there is no such thing
as a genuine smile
when i haven't truly laughed
in a quite a while

and i can't believe anyone
when they tell me that they care
i just don't know anymore
everything is so unfair

and i fear there's no escape
no easy way out
i fear there is no one left turn to
i can't even cry aloud

smoke and mirrors

there is silence
there is *always* silence

in those quiet moments is when the ugly truth bares its wicked
teeth and tells her to hate herself

a liar
a thief
a heartbreaker

a life full of people who will never really *know*.

each day, each face she wears is a fraudulent story
weaved by a tongue which tastes of silver
it is her truth, that which she cannot face
she doesn't have the courage to do that, not yet
maybe she never will
nothing but cracked mirrors and shattered tears

maybe one day, death steals her, someone will find
all her old, dry parchment, so untended
they'll read the scribbles like unsent love letters

ink caressed skin, blank white page

there is sunlight, but there is not always sunlight
which she is grateful for because her fear lives in the dark
and she belongs to it, fester.

FISH

i was told not to teach you your name.
reborn at three years old.
there were always reasons why we weren't sisters.
half my blood, all my heart.
but then they locked who you were away,
part of me by extension.

you became someone new.
they rewrote the pages we had scribbled.
not all the parts were beautiful.
but the parts where you smiled don't fade.
now you'll never be that person again.

i know that you don't understand.
but what of the day when you do?
then what shall I say?
you're two people and one.
you're here but you've been changed.
we have a shared history, and the weight of that is mine to bear
alone, for now.
they ripped you from our mother's womb.
bled the parts of her in you, from our open wounds.

well...my mother, not yours.
not really anymore.
because the proof of who I am is in my hands.
while yours are empty.
but I'm here for you
always.

"

i was told not to teach you your name.
This line begins the story of my sister's identity changing through
adoption. When she was little, we used to say her name to her and have
her repeat it back. When one of our social workers noticed after an
adoption plan was made, they took us aside and said it was a good idea
to stop, because her name was changing soon.

I have lost track of the number of times these 'little asks' that were so
loaded were dropped on me so casually…

This poem was written shortly after I learned that birth certificates get
changed when legal adoptions occur. A foundational, meaningless lie
about our identities. Telling my biological mom that her daughter's
birth certificate has another woman's name on it…

"I'm nothing, they made me nothing."

I can't explain the way those words hit me when she said them.

the heart that silence built.

i stand on the threshold
pouring out the liquid from this ... glass until it is half full.
i have to look at it this way, half full

because if i don't when i'm around you all i'll be able to feel is the
emptiness.
this chasm separating me from you
you started digging before i even got here and even though i've
begged you so many times to put down the shovel you keep
moving the dirt

sometimes i look into that hole and imagine myself down there
except now that i'm there you're moving the dirt back in
burying the parts that you don't like to see so that you don't have
to look at them
forgetting who i am, putting a picture on the mantle piece that is
a version of me that you can accept

don't you ever notice it?
the puddle at the door every time you step outside
or maybe that's what i'm getting wrong here
you never go outside
which is why you'll never look at the world in a different way
which is why this is where I begin, and you end
which is why every time i try to take another step in your
direction i'm hacking off another limb

you've painted the walls of your house the colour of silence.
when you did it, you handed me the roller and asked me to help
and I didn't think to say no

because I thought it will just be easier this way

it's not easier this way,
but I can't get the taste of your soil out of the back of my mouth
and the colour off of my skin and so all I can manage to do is
turn away...
open my ears while you demand i keep quiet
that i just accept this, your hands laden with stones.

somehow that's how you control this
by holding them out in front of me while claiming you won't use
them but to be honest,
i don't quite believe you

the broken ipod

at the threshold i split myself in half
how else will i fit into the silence that you ask me to perform?

it's not an easy process
carried out by hack saw and unskilled hands
practiced but dispassionate
repetition without truth is only a tired task

we're stuck in this cycle
where i show up torn and bloody and you ask why so much of
me is missing.
you ask why so much of me is missing
you ask why so much of me is missing
what answer can i give you that you want to hear?
your tongue and your unspoken expectation has created this
my complacency has created this
my fear has created this

i stand at this street corner
cradling a cigarette under an umbrella
i only smoke when it's raining

the first time i dropped my iPod classic
i took it to the store and they told me
that i dropped it in such a way
i damaged one of the few things that can break it
otherwise it's the sturdiest iPod of all of them

i think about this and i wish
that you had only held me
a bit more tenderly

people can't relate to lizard man

no concept of time
i check the yes box
under family history of mental health

my mother in the hospital bed
black mouth
fucked up father
typical

follow up papers
i google suicidal ideations
i check no
i lie/d

sitting at the top of the staircase
locked roof access
12
counting the pills
maybe the night to sleep forever
17
soft red lines in the bathtub
21

i didn't mean to lie

blurred timelines
when was the first indication of...
have you been diagnosed for...
no
counting scars
morning panic

afternoon panic
evening panic

late night 'you have been so weak'
it might be just tonight
or it might be the scars i'm counting

when was the first time you went to therapy?
grade 4
grade 8
work place
ending relationships

i'm trying to tell her there is something more
but the words never come
just the lie
just the check mark under 'no'

are you waiting for me to fall asleep?
are you waiting for me to never wake up?

dear 4am
please, i just...
...can't

moon poem

she,
hangs in the sky
half alight

hangs in the balance
half of herself

with nothing but the emptiness to consume her

the hardest day

on the hardest day
you, were the only one who saw me

on the hardest day…
they sent me back to school
they sent me back to school as if nothing happened

a footnote in the notes of my worker
unmentioned by my caregivers
unrecognized by my new life
alone, without my mother, too wrapped up in her own grief
called lucky for missing geography
called delinquent for missing geography
who the fuck cares about geography
when there is no ground beneath my feet

this…funeral
that nobody would call a funeral
that nobody would let me mourn or scream or cry or just
end.

everything stopped, and everything kept going
…but not you

you sat here with me
in this empty car,
where she used to be with me
in this empty life,
where she used to be with me

it shouldn't have even been you
but i guess no one else cared enough to give me a lift to the
funeral

you were the only one who wore black
you were the only who stopped
you were the only one who said
"this is isn't fair
and i'm here for you
as long as you need"

you who listened to my poems,
you who kept coming back for the one nobody cared about
you...saw me
maybe because,
you yourself had just been to a funeral

death, took you from me
from this world
and they told me i wasn't supposed to mourn you either
that you weren't important enough
but all the supposedly important people weren't there for me on
the hardest day

this is something that i never got to say for you
so I will say it for myself,
and hope that *just maybe*, you can hear it too

thank you,
the gift you gave me on the hardest day
has carried me through all the days that have followed it
i can't say for sure,
that i would be here without you
you, who saw me when no one else would look.

"

This was written about Dan, whom I mentioned earlier in the book with the poem "Dave". After my sister, mother and I had our final visit before my sister was to be adopted (at the time I had every reason to believe that this was the last time we would be together), I was scheduled to go back to school, as if it was any other day.

Upon arriving at my school, Dan pulled over and said to me that he'd made sure he had no more drives lined up that day, and that I could stay in the car as long as I wanted before returning to school...

It's one of the kindest, most attuned gestures I have ever experienced in my life.

there's no scripts

there are people in my life that i have entire conversations with
in my head
sometimes i just get carried away by a thought
sometimes because I need to rehearse
either way it's driven by the panic
the anticipation of knowing i'm at the precipice of a cliff and this
next word will be what throws me off it

"i need you," i say unexpectedly
the truth rocks through me, inescapable and I begin to cry

when i tell them "i'm engaged," they look at my hand.
"there's no ring," i say,
that's not something I've ever wanted
they smile and nod

when she speaks to me she assumes i agree
i bite my tongue and look away
perhaps she fills the silence with what she wants to hear
looking in the other direction

there are only so many vacant eyes i can look into before i
break.

"will you marry me?" i say
it's Wednesday and we are sitting on the living room couch.
i have to leave soon and though it's not like anything i've seen at
the movies
it's exactly what I wanted

"we're grieved," they say

disappointed and wearing the mask of what's best for me
just because it's true for them, doesn't make it any less painful
for me

"you're my best friend," you say
we talk about the future and the sex we had last night

"they'll never know me," i say
i want them to
you see this with startling clarity.
sometimes i think the truth is more important than the fallout
than the racing heart and shaking hands
than the distance it creates

"this is hard sometimes," we say
both ultimately knowing it's worth it

i hadn't been looking for the one,
but i revel in how well we fit
how similarly we want
how together we dream

"i can't do this anymore," i say
yet still you stay and hold me

i don't need this to be well written
i just need it to be true

po·lar·i·ty

/pəˈlerədē,pōˈlerədē/
the property of having poles or being polar.
the state of having two opposite or contradictory tendencies,
opinions, or aspects.

destruction & creation

"I'll wreck this if I have to
Tell me, what good would that do?
It's getting better in the worst way"
- Masterpiece Theater III, Mariana's Trench

one day

the mourning after
it's a beautiful day
with an unsettled wind that just won't quit
it's perfect

it was THE day to cross
"wake & bake & Starbucks"
off my self care wellness menu
i even put on a cute outfit.

i ate a croissant
alone on a bench
heard smoke signals
and saw a Pride Flag waving in the distance.

i remember a night in Florida like this
you turned to a little girl and said
"we'll all be a family together one day,"
i wonder what happened to that one day
or who dreamed it up to begin with

excavation

silence
reverberating through the sinew of my muscles and the marrow
of my bones
there are no words
no words for this moment
no words for the short but arduous journey that brought us here
a buried path that seems to extend further than what we can see

we'll excavate it one day

a sigh of relief
my secrets are almost done being kept
a stuttering hello
a nervous laugh

i remember when you cried 11 years ago
i remember when you cried 13 years ago

you didn't know it then but I collected your tears and saved them
in a jar
a forgotten ache
an unnameable distrust
polaroid heart, taking pictures of the memories
everything that has brought us here
to this moment

scrap booking a life they wanted hidden
they say 'not insecure'
they say 'don't complicate it'
they say 'don't speak'
but this don't ask don't tell silence

but this way that you asked anyways
this way I bit my tongue, hard and swallowed the blood without
notice

they say 'sorry'
but the damage is done

the narrative I haven't told you yet is that I almost didn't make it
hole punched fingertips
empty frames and hollow hooks
half a sister
now I speak

are you done searching?
or have you only just begun?

destruction & creation

the things i had lost cannot be replaced...*always*
there is searching for meaning in a world that is empty without
you
a ghost led me down a gravel road, far from where i came to be
without questions, i moved forward no longer afraid of the past

begin again

to our excavation little ones...

"

The poetry book is dedicated to my sister.
To everyone you have been, to who you are today and
to who you are becoming.

Acknowledgements

It's hard to know where even to begin.

First I think I would like to thank my partner in crime, Owen Seto, for his support in helping me edit this book (this would have been a hopeless task on my own). And also his support in all things...I love you.

There is a poet who came before me, who breathed life into me. Who taught me my love of nature and mountains. Who taught me to be curious and compassionate. Who taught me how to stand on my own, to be a wild woman. To laugh loudly and not care so much about what others think. She is my mother, and I give thanks to her for this journey of life.

To my little FISH, to my sister. To all you are and will be, thank you for holding space for me to publish this book. Thank you for your fire, and everything you give to the world. For your understanding and compassion through everything that has happened. For your love.

There are two writers who inspired me to publish my poetry. My friend and mentor, Andrea Gunraj, author of The Lost Sister. Fellow adoptee, advocate and friend, Nathan Ross, author of Mourning After the Storm. Thank you for your courage, and for sparking a flame in me.

Another special thank you to Aviva Zukerman-Schure, Kate Mannion and Chloe Hockley from Never Too Late at the Adoption Council of Ontario. I am not sure this book would have been possible without the personal support I have received from you during a significant time of loss, healing and changing.

I am so grateful, and so honoured to donate a portion of the profits of this book to Never Too Late.

Special thank you also to Dianne Mathes, Executive Director of the Adoption Council of Ontario, and Kathy Soden, PACT Program Manager. Your enthusiasm, compassion, support and encouragement have been meaningful to me for as long as I have known you. Thank you also for supporting the publishing of this book and allowing me to share it with the Adoption Council of Ontario and its audience. I hope that this platform helps it find its way to someone that will find some meaning in it.

To adoptees everywhere, thank you for sharing your voices and your stories. Thank you for helping me to understand myself, and to not feel so alone on this journey. If this book brings you anything close to that, I will be so honoured.

To my adoption community at large...thank you for your hope that everything would work out, that things would get better, even though it was misguided and misplaced.

To parents through adoption and other less traditional family-making methods who never stop learning...thank you.

To everyone in my chosen family, thank you.

Finally, the most important thank you is to myself. To my inner child for surviving and to my adult self for carving out a different path. For rejecting making myself small for the comfort of those around me. For setting boundaries and doing arduous healing work. Here is to becoming a badass psychotherapist.

"I've been feeling
Inside out in my feelings

Upside down, on the ceiling
I'm finally breathing
The smoke ain't gone, but it's clearing
I ain't there yet, but I'm healing"
- Healing, Fletcher